TALES OF

Greek Mythology II

RETOLD TIMELESS CLASSICS

Perfection Learning®

Retold by L. L. Owens

Editor: Paula Reece
Illustrator: Greg Hargreaves
Designer: Jan M. Michalson

For information, contact
Perfection Learning® Corporation
1000 North Second Avenue, P.O. Box 500
Logan, Iowa 51546-1099.
Phone: 800-831-4190 • Fax: 712-644-2392

Paperback ISBN 0-7891-5064-6
Cover Craft® ISBN 0-7807-9035-9
Printed in the U.S.A.

Contents

THE MIDAS TOUCH

A tale based on Nathaniel Hawthorne's
version of this legend.

There once was a very rich king named
Midas. He ruled over Phrygia in ancient
Greece. He was also an avid gardener. And his
favorite thing in the whole world was gold.
Next, of course, to his daughter Marygold.

Now King Midas had lots of gold. But not
enough to suit him. He planned to gather as
much gold as his palace would hold.

"I'm doing this for you, Marygold," he
explained. "I must provide for your future."

The simple truth was that he loved the mere
thought of gold. He loved the sight of gold.
He loved the feel of gold. He even loved the
smell of gold. It was even sweeter than the
scent of his prized roses.

And so he bought gold everywhere he went. He bought gold jewelry, sculptures, and furniture. Soon he ran out of room. So he created an underground chamber that held more gold. Whenever King Midas felt sad, he visited his special room. The mounds of glistening gold always cheered him right up.

"What could be more beautiful?" he wondered aloud. Then he quickly added, "Other than my precious Marygold, of course!"

Still, Midas wanted more gold. More gold than he had ever seen. More gold than he could possibly imagine.

A WISH COMES TRUE

One day, Midas was frustrated. He'd run out of nearby places from which to buy gold. He shook his fist at the heavens. He cried, "I need more gold!"

Suddenly, the god Dionysus appeared. He had a bright smile. "You wish for more gold, King Midas?"

"Why, yes, indeed," Midas answered. "I've bought all the gold in the surrounding kingdoms. Now I must send my men to faraway lands."

"Oh, my," declared Dionysus. "That will surely take a while. Wouldn't you rather have more gold right away?"

"Naturally!" said Midas. He bent down and picked up a rock. "Why, I wish I could just turn this rock to gold. It would make things so much easier. Can you help?"

"I can," said Dionysus. "All you have to do is repeat your wish. But first, I want you to think about it. Think about it carefully."

Midas paused. Slowly, he said, "I wish everything that I touch would change to gold!"

"Are you certain? Have you thought it through?"

"I am certain!"

"Very well. I shall grant your wish. Tomorrow at sunrise, you shall gain the Golden Touch."

In the blink of an eye, Dionysus was gone. But Midas barely noticed. He was too busy rushing to his bedroom. On the way, he sang—

"Early to bed! Early to rise! I'll have the Golden Touch at the next sunrise!"

The king slept soundly. Much like a happy child. The next morning, the sun peeked over the hills. Midas sprang out of bed. He was eager to test his new gift.

Midas touched a chair. Nothing happened. Then he reached for his dressing gown. Again, nothing.

"Was it all a dream?" he wondered aloud. He walked around the room, touching everything in sight.

Finally, he sat down to rest. "It must have been a dream," he said sadly. "Either that or a cruel, cruel joke."

Midas quietly watched the sun rise ever higher. His room was still rather dark.

"I'll rest for a bit longer," he sighed. "Then I'll put this foolishness out of my mind."

Little by little, the sky became brighter. It wasn't long before a single ray of bright sunlight shone through the king's window— directly on his face.

"Time for breakfast," Midas said. He stood up and put on his royal clothes. Then he noticed something—

The chair had turned to gold. And so had his clothes! They were now made of a shimmering fabric spun from fine gold threads.

"Aha!" he cried. "The sunbeam on my face activated my gift! I'm rich! I'm rich! I'm the richest king who ever lived!"

Midas danced about the palace. Everything he touched turned to gold. Then he frolicked about the palace grounds. He touched the trees. They turned to gold. He ran his fingers across blades of grass. They turned to gold. He tapped his favorite garden statues. They turned to gold. He cradled his beautiful roses. They, too, turned to gold.

EVERYTHING King Midas touched turned to gold!

The king was delighted. His dreams had come true. He would be forever surrounded by gold.

BREAKFAST IN THE GARDEN

All this running to and fro had made Midas hungry. So he sat at his garden table and ordered breakfast by ringing a bell. His chair and table quickly turned to gold. So did the bell.

Just then, little Marygold came bouncing to the table.

Midas was happy to see her, as usual. "Good morning, dear child," said he.

"Good morning, Father," Marygold replied.

A servant brought out the breakfast tray. He served Marygold first, for those were his orders. Then he poured coffee for the king.

Midas drank from his now golden cup.

"Aaaaaarrgghh!" he cried, obviously in pain. The coffee had turned to molten gold as soon as it crossed his lips.

"What's the matter, Father?" asked Marygold.

"Nothing, my child," Midas replied. He was determined not to let anything ruin his good mood.

Midas studied the breakfast food for a moment. He wondered how he'd be able to eat. Then he had an idea. Swiftly, he grabbed a potato and tried to gobble it down. But he was not quick enough. The potato stuck fast in his throat. Midas began to choke!

He turned red in the face. And he pounded his chest. At last, he was able to cough. And the golden spud flew to the ground.

Marygold rushed to her father's side. "Oh, Father!" she cried. She flung her arms around his neck.

"Marygold—no!" he roared, trying to twist out of her grasp. But it was too late. He felt his darling daughter's arms go stiff.

Carefully, Midas lifted Marygold to the ground. Her golden eyes were frozen wide open.

ALL THAT GLITTERS

"What have I done?" cried Midas. He caressed his daughter's cheek.

"Oh, Marygold! I've lost you! And all because of my foolish wish. How could I have been so stupid? If I could just have you back . . . If I could just pinch your rosy cheeks . . . If I could just hear your sweet voice . . . I'd gladly be the poorest man in the world."

Midas stared at Marygold for the rest of the day. He desperately tried to think of a solution. Night fell and Midas continued to stare. The moonlight flickered across little Marygold's golden figure. And Midas sank deep into despair.

The birds began to chirp at daybreak. Midas had not moved from his post. Presently, he sensed that someone was behind him. He turned around.

Dionysus was there.

"Hello, King Midas," Dionysus began. His smile was still as bright as the sun. "Are you enjoying the Golden Touch?"

Midas met his gaze with sad, weary eyes. He said, "I am in misery."

"I don't understand," replied Dionysus. "I granted your wish. Is the Golden Touch not working?"

"It is working," Midas admitted.

"Then don't you have everything that your heart desired? Doesn't everything you touch turn to gold?" asked Dionysus.

Midas snapped, "Gold is not everything! *Marygold* was the only thing my heart truly cared for."

"Ah!" exclaimed Dionysus. "It seems you have learned something since yesterday."

"I certainly have."

"Let me test you, then," said Dionysus. "Tell me something. Which is worth more—a golden goblet or one cup of clear, cold water?"

"The water, of course!" exclaimed the king. "Gold cannot quench my thirst!"

"A brick of gold?" continued Dionysus. "Or a crust of bread?"

"The bread! The bread!" answered Midas. "It is worth all the gold on Earth!"

"A golden statue? Or your own little Marygold?"

"Marygold!" cried Midas. "I would not have given her up for anything. Not even for the power of changing the world into a solid lump of gold!"

Dionysus studied Midas. Finally he noted, "You are wiser than you once were. Tell me what you have learned."

"I learned that water and bread and my child are more valuable than all the riches in the world. And I learned that possessions cannot create happiness."

"Good!" said Dionysus. "I must know one more thing. Do you sincerely wish to rid yourself of the Golden Touch?"

"More than anything!" replied Midas.

"Away with you, then," said Dionysus. "Go plunge into the river that runs past your garden. Take a vase with you and fill it with the river's water. Then sprinkle it over anything you'd like to change back from gold. Do so with all good intentions. And you may repair the damage caused by your greed."

King Midas bowed humbly before Dionysus. He rose to say thank you. But Dionysus was already gone.

Quickly, Midas grabbed a pitcher from the table. He ran toward the river. With each step, he left behind a path of gold. He reached the river's edge and jumped in. He kicked around underwater for a moment.

When he surfaced, his clothes were no longer gold. Neither was the pitcher he'd been holding.

He filled the pitcher and got out of the river. He was about to run to Marygold's side. Then he decided to make sure the Golden Touch was gone. He noticed a violet growing on the riverbank. He reached down and touched it. The flower remained as delicate and purple as ever.

It was the prettiest flower he had ever seen. Midas had never really appreciated the beauty in such small things before. But all that was changing.

"At last!" he cried gleefully. "The curse of the Golden Touch has been lifted! Now I can rescue my dear Marygold."

When he reached his daughter, he sprinkled handfuls of the water over her. Her rosy cheeks and warm smile came back to life.

"Oh, Father!" she giggled. "You're sprinkling water all over my new dress!" She had no memory of being turned to gold.

Midas embraced his daughter. "Come with me, my child," he said. "I must fix the garden. Along with everything else I touched."

The king sprinkled water everywhere. Soon the palace and the gardens were back to normal. And Midas went back to the business of being a king—and a doting father to Marygold.

As life went on, King Midas sometimes thought about the Golden Touch. He remembered it when he was near the river. For its sands now sparkled like gold. He also remembered it when he looked at Marygold. For now her chestnut curls shimmered with a few golden streaks.

Midas eventually grew old. He spent glorious days admiring his rose gardens. And playing with Marygold's twins—one boy and one girl.

Sometimes, he'd bounce the tots on his knee. He loved to tell them stories. Especially about the Golden Touch.

He'd tell a splendid tale. Then he'd stroke the children's golden curls. He'd say:

"To this day, I hate the very sight of all gold—except this!"

Aphrodite and Her Beloved Adonis

Aphrodite was playing with her son, Eros. She watched him practice with his bow and arrow. He was very young, so his aim wasn't the best.

"Try to hit the tree," suggested Aphrodite. She thought the large trunk would make an excellent target.

"Which tree?" Eros asked.

"The one to my left," Aphrodite pointed.

Eros took careful aim. Then he released his arrow. It sailed through the air. It missed the tree. And it pierced Aphrodite's heart!

Aphrodite felt no pain. For she was a goddess. But the wound was quite deep. As it healed, Aphrodite was surprised when a youth named Adonis sprang forth from her flesh.

He was the most beautiful creature Aphrodite had ever seen. She could not take her eyes off him. From then on, she could not bear to be away from him.

Aphrodite had always loved to spend lazy afternoons lying in the shade. She did this wherever she was—Paphos, Amanthos, even Mount Olympus. But suddenly, she stopped visiting all her favorite spots.

Instead, she dressed like the huntress Artemis. And she followed Adonis on his hunts. Then in hopes of pleasing the young man, she hunted too. Just rabbits and other gentle animals, mind you. She was afraid of bears and wolves and such.

One day, Aphrodite noticed Adonis hunting a bear. She issued an order. Adonis was to stay away from large prey.

She said, "It is not safe for you to hunt such huge animals. Remember, your youth and beauty will not charm bloodthirsty beasts. I must insist that you hunt small animals only. They cannot hurt you."

"But it takes more courage to hunt dangerous prey," protested Adonis. "And I am very courageous."

"I know, dear Adonis. But don't you see? My happiness is at stake. If you get hurt, I will be lost. And it will be your fault."

"Then I won't get hurt," Adonis declared.

"Enough!" Aphrodite warned. "Do not question me. Or you will end up like Atalanta and Hippomenes!"

Well, Adonis had heard of those poor souls. They had angered Aphrodite. And she had turned them into lions.

Adonis did not reply.

Aphrodite said, "Good. Then it is settled. By the way, I must travel to Cyprus today. But I will come back to you tomorrow."

"Have a good trip," said Adonis.

Aphrodite's chariot—drawn by swans—arrived. She climbed in and rode away. She called back over her shoulder—

"Adonis! See that you heed my warning!"

Moments later, Adonis's dogs started barking. They had found a wild boar. It had been asleep in its lair. Now it was very angry.

As the boar attacked the dogs, Adonis threw his spear. He hit the boar in the neck.

"I am sorry, Aphrodite," Adonis said into the air. "I really have no choice right now."

With its teeth, the boar ripped the spear from its neck. It rushed at Adonis, snorting and puffing as it ran.

Adonis tried to run away. But the boar was too swift. The boar trapped Adonis and plunged its tusks into Adonis's stomach.

Meanwhile, Aphrodite was still in her chariot. She was just outside Cyprus when she heard a hideous groan. It echoed across the earth and filled Aphrodite with dread.

"Adonis!" she shrieked. To the swans, she cried, "Turn back! Hurry!"

Soon the chariot landed at the bloody scene. It was too late. Adonis was dead.

Aphrodite was overcome with grief. She threw herself over Adonis's lifeless body. She wept bitterly.

To the Fates, she said—

"I command you to create a tribute to my grief. One that shall be renewed each year. Forevermore."

The Fates replied—
"As you wish, Aphrodite."

Aphrodite cupped Adonis's blood in her hands. She lifted her hands high above her head. Then the Fates laced the blood with nectar. Aphrodite sprinkled the mixture over the earth.

Instantly, a strong gust of wind blew Adonis into the heavens. Then the air was still. A beautiful blood-red flower sprang forth from the ground. It was called the Wind Flower.

The Wind Flower blooms every spring. But it dies young—just like Adonis. As soon as the blossoms open up, the wind blows the petals away.

The Legends of
Echo and Narcissus

Part I—The Wood Nymph Echo

Echo was a lovely nymph. She spent endless happy days in the woods. She was gifted at all woodland sports. So much so that the goddess Artemis took her under her wing.

"She is an excellent huntress," Artemis remarked. "Even if she does chatter on a bit."

Echo was quite talkative, you see. She had a dreadful habit of always having the last word in any chat. She did so in arguments too.

One day, Hera was looking for Zeus. The gods were meeting at Zeus's palace on Olympus. Zeus was late. And Hera was none too pleased. She suspected he was in the forest.

"He is probably entertaining the nymphs with his stories again," she guessed. So she followed his usual path.

Soon Hera saw Echo. She called to her, "Have you seen my husband?"

Echo Makes a Decision

Now Echo could tell that Hera was angry. She knew Zeus was in the clearing with some of the nymphs. And she did not want her nymph friends to get in trouble. So she tried to stall Hera. She rambled on about nothing. Until Hera lost her patience.

Hera said, "I must go, Echo. Good-bye."

"Good-bye, Hera," said Echo. "I wish you could stay and talk a while longer."

"I cannot. If you see Zeus, tell him I'm looking for him," Hera said.

"I'll do that. *If* I see Zeus, that is. Although I doubt that I will."

"Thank you," Hera replied. And she began to walk away.

"It's just that you never know when Zeus will visit the forest," Echo continued.

"Right," said Hera, still walking away.

"He's so important, you know. We nymphs are honored when he calls upon us."

Hera waved without turning back.

Echo raised her voice. "There's no need to check the clearing!" she called. "No one is likely to be there today. If I were you, I would turn around and go home."

Hera didn't respond at all. She neared the edge of the clearing.

Echo tried again. "Hera!" she cried. "Turn back! I think I see Zeus coming from the other direction!"

It was too late. Hera had spotted Zeus. It was just as she had guessed. He was relaxing in the clearing. And he was charming the nymphs with tales of the gods.

Hera angrily called to Zeus. "Where have you been? It's time for the gods' feast!"

Zeus chuckled. "Ah, my dear wife. Thank you for reminding me. I will fly up to the palace at once." He snapped his fingers and was gone. His big voice boomed over the woods.

"See that you join me at once, my dear."

But Hera had something to take care of first.

Hera Punishes Echo

Hera approached poor Echo, wagging a finger.

"You!" she cried. "You knew where Zeus was. And you tried to delay me with your words! But it didn't work!"

"I am so sorry," said Echo. "I meant no harm."

"Silence!" Hera shrieked. "Do not speak unless I command it."

"Yes, Hera."

"I said SILENCE! Not one word! *No* speaking!" Hera paused to see if she'd made her point.

A frightened Echo stared back at Hera. She couldn't help herself. "Yes, Hera," she said eagerly. "I understand. I will not speak until you command it. Not one peep!"

"That's it!" Hera said with disgust. "I shall teach you a lesson."

Echo said, "Wha—?"

Hera placed a hand over the nymph's mouth. She said, "You shall continue to have the last word. But you shall no longer be able to speak first. And you may only repeat the words spoken to you."

And so it was from that day forward.

Echo Meets Narcissus

It was a sunny day. Echo was walking through the mountains. And she saw young Narcissus for the first time. He was so beautiful! Echo fell madly in love. She followed him—secretly—as he hiked. She hid among the trees.

I wish I could speak to him, Echo thought. I long to tell him how I feel!

Narcissus sensed that someone was near. He called out, "Who is out there?"

Echo replied, "Who is out there?"

Narcissus said, "Show yourself to me."

Echo responded in kind.

Narcissus was confused. "Why do you mock me?" he asked.

"Why do you mock me?" was Echo's answer.

"Please, miss," Narcissus began. "Let us meet."

When Echo repeated his words, Narcissus was annoyed. Echo then stepped out from behind a tree. She held open her arms and approached the young man.

But Narcissus backed away. "Away with you!" he shouted. "I'd sooner die than be with you!"

Naturally, the only words Echo could muster just made things worse. Narcissus stormed off. He continued his trek up the mountain. He'd climbed rather high when he spotted Echo far below. She still stood where he'd left her. She was hoping for another chance to speak with him.

"I hope you turn to stone!" Narcissus shouted.

After a slight delay, Echo repeated, "I hope you turn to stone!" By this time, tears were streaming down her cheeks. She knew what the young man must think of her. But she was powerless to change his mind.

I wish I would turn to stone, she thought. Then I would be spared the shame of others' cruel judgments. Besides, I have nothing left to live for. I have already lost my one true love.

Echo continued to stand very still. Slowly, over many years, her flesh and bones faded away. Until she was part of the rocks—part of the mountain.

Echo's voice remained, though. As it does to this day. Whenever someone calls out in the mountains, she is ready with her reply.

And she always has the last word.

Part II—Narcissus the Beautiful

Narcissus had believed that Echo was rude. But you may have noticed that he took no time to question her odd behavior. He simply assumed the worst.

He was incredibly vain. He felt he was the best-looking boy who ever lived. And he was used to hearing compliments day in and day out. He was also used to nymphs falling in love with him at first glance.

Echo hadn't responded to him the way others had. So Narcissus was more than just offended by her actions. He was sure that Echo was crazy!

Someone Is Watching

For some time now, Nemesis had been watching Narcissus. She followed his actions from on high. She decided, after much study, that the boy's life was going too smoothly.

"Things come so easily to him," she mused. "Yet he does nothing to truly deserve his good fortune. He is far too vain and boastful. I must do something to correct this problem."

She thought for a while. Then she laughed. "Tee-hee-hee! I have the perfect plan for Narcissus!"

One day soon after, Narcissus was hunting. Nemesis saw to it that he grew tired and thirsty. When he came upon a pool of water, he stopped to rest. Nemesis's plan had been set in motion.

The Art of Reflection

The glassy water in the pool was clean and pure. It looked untouched by nature. Narcissus knelt to take a drink. A beautiful water spirit winked back at him.

"Why, hello!" said a stunned Narcissus. "You are such a fine-looking creature!"

There was no answer, of course. For Narcissus was looking—and cooing—at his own image.

For hours, Narcissus stared at his reflection. He listed the many fair features he saw.

"What big, beautiful eyes you have," he murmured.

With glee, he noted, "Those curls! They are as smooth as Apollo's!"

"Ah, such high cheekbones," he said admiringly. "And those charming lips!"

He was in love with himself, and he didn't even know it!

Finally, Narcissus reached out to the image. It reached out to him too. But when Narcissus tried to touch it, it disappeared. And Narcissus got wet.

He dried his arm and looked again. The water image had returned. It smiled up at Narcissus, just as Narcissus smiled down at it.

Narcissus found it impossible to break his gaze.

I'd better not try to embrace it again, he thought. I'd hate to lose it once more!

He no longer cared about resting. Or eating. Or hunting. All he thought about was admiring the image. It consumed his body and mind.

Narcissus began to fade into his surroundings. Just as Echo had before him. Over time, Narcissus lost his beauty and, eventually, his life.

As Narcissus drew his last breath, his shadow paused over the silvery pool. It stole a final glimpse of the once-perfect face.

Nemesis, who'd been watching all along, was satisfied. "He got what he deserved," she said.

The nymphs were sad to hear that Narcissus had died. They asked Nemesis to create a beautiful flower in his honor.

"He earned that much for his lesson," agreed Nemesis. And that is how the purple-and-white blooming Narcissus came to be.

OEDIPUS AND THE ORACLE

A boy was born to King Laius of Thebes. Soon the king received a warning. An oracle said—

"You must kill your newborn son. It is the only way to save yourself. It is the only way to save the throne. And it is the only way to save your people."

Laius knew there was no time to waste. After all, an oracle had spoken! So he quickly found a shepherd. He handed him the baby.

"Take this child!" he ordered. "Destroy him at once."

"Destroy him?" replied the gentle shepherd. He shook his head in disbelief. "He is a mere infant, sir."

"Do you dare question your king?" Laius barked.

"No, sir," said the shepherd.

"Good!" cried Laius. He walked away without ever looking back. The shepherd couldn't tell that the king's heart was breaking.

The shepherd wondered what to do. He did not wish to kill the boy. But he had to obey King Laius. At least in part, he reasoned.

He came up with a plan. "I'll tie him to this tree," he said. "Perhaps someone will find him. If I leave the field, no one will know where the boy came from. And I won't know who takes him."

The shepherd tied the baby—by one foot— to the branch of an olive tree. Then he scurried away.

At dusk, a peasant was passing by the olive tree. He heard a baby screaming. He saw the poor boy tied to the tree. The man rushed to untie him.

"My goodness!" he exclaimed. "What have we here?"

The man tended to the infant's swollen foot. The child calmed down in the peasant's arms.

"I think I can help you, dear boy," the peasant said gently. "I come from Corinth. My king and queen long for a baby. They are kind people, and I know they will take you in."

The peasant carried the baby to Corinth. He was right—his King Polybus and Queen Merope loved the child instantly. They decided to raise him as their own.

"What shall we name him?" asked the new mother. She was very excited.

Polybus replied, "Let's call him Oedipus." That meant "swollen foot" in their language.

"Oedipus it is," agreed Merope. And she sang her son to sleep.

Many years passed. Oedipus grew up happy and strong. Polybus and Merope loved him and cared for him. They never told him that he was not their son by birth. But soon they wished they had. For someone else beat them to it.

"I heard about your parents!" laughed the village idiot.

"What do you mean?" asked Oedipus.

"The king and queen are NOT your real mother and father."

"You are foolish, indeed!" Oedipus replied.

The idiot said simply, "Ask them."

And ask them Oedipus did.

"Are you my real parents?" Oedipus believed in getting to the point.

"Why do you ask, son?" said Polybus.

"I want an answer," Oedipus demanded. "Mother? Have you anything to say?"

Merope couldn't lie. "You were brought to us when you were an infant. You were a gift. We loved you from the start."

"Why didn't you tell me?" he asked.

"We didn't think it mattered," said Polybus. "Besides, you were abandoned—left for dead. We wanted to protect you from the truth. We didn't want you to feel unwanted."

Oedipus quickly forgave his parents. He was grateful that they had given him such a good life. Yet he was still curious about his birth parents. So he set out to find them.

"I hope you understand," he told Merope. "I must go."

"I understand," said Merope. "I shall miss you."

"I shall miss you too, son," said Polybus. He shook his son's hand. Then he and Merope watched him drive away.

"Do you think we will ever see him again?" Merope asked Polybus.

"Only time will tell, Merope."

OEDIPUS'S FATEFUL DECISION

Oedipus began his search by consulting the oracle at Delphi. The oracle said—

"Do not search for your parents. If you find them, your father will die by your hand. And you will marry your mother."

"That's ridiculous!" Oedipus replied. He had been taught to believe the oracle. But this time, he just couldn't.

"I speak the truth," said the oracle. "No good can come from this quest. Pain and destruction will haunt you forever. Leave it in the past."

"But I would never kill my own father," said Oedipus. "Never."

"The story is written on the wind."

"Then I shall have to change the story," said Oedipus.

With that, he moved on. He was more determined than ever to find his parents— and prove the oracle wrong.

Meanwhile, King Laius was traveling to Delphi. One loyal servant traveled with him. The road was narrow. They met other people here and there. Most were traveling in the opposite direction.

On the second morning, Laius and his servant met a young man driving a chariot.

The servant called out the king's order. "Yield to King Laius!"

The fellow did not hear the command. So he did no such thing. Laius responded by killing one of the stranger's horses.

The young man was enraged. "I'll teach you to challenge Oedipus!" he bellowed. Then he slew the king. When he turned to kill the servant, the servant was gone. He had fled on horseback and was hurrying home to Thebes.

Oedipus did not know that he had just murdered a king. He certainly had no idea the king was his own father! So he buried Laius by the side of the road. "Poor old fool!" he muttered. "You should never have killed my horse."

OEDIPUS CHALLENGES THE SPHINX

The servant arrived back at the palace the next day. He went straight to Queen Jocasta and told her the bad news.

"He is dead, my queen," said the servant. "King Laius is dead."

"No!" screamed Jocasta. "Not my dear husband!"

He went on to describe what had happened. He was feeling a bit cowardly for fleeing. So he claimed that a large band of robbers had stopped them. And that he had escaped only after a long fight.

The queen was heartbroken. But she would have no time to grieve. After the servant left, her advisers arrived. They had yet more bad news to share.

They told Jocasta of a fierce monster. This monster was called the Sphinx. She had the head of a woman and the body of a lion. She had heard of the king's death. So she traveled to Thebes to begin menacing his people.

The Sphinx had positioned herself atop a huge boulder outside Thebes. She was stopping all travelers coming in and out of the city.

To each traveler, she posed a riddle. If the traveler solved the riddle, the Sphinx granted safe passage. All others were killed on the spot. She showed no mercy.

So far, no one had been able to enter or leave Thebes. The riddles were difficult. And the bodies were piling up near the Sphinx's rock.

Oedipus finally reached Thebes' entrance. Something had drawn him to this great city. He had already been warned about the mighty Sphinx. But he was unafraid.

"What is your riddle?" he shouted to the monster.

The Sphinx was prepared. She asked—

"Which animal travels on four feet in the morning? Two feet at midday? And three feet in the evening?"

The Sphinx was pleased with her question. She thought it was quite tricky.

But Oedipus knew the answer right away. He said, "Man is the animal you describe. He crawls on his hands and knees as a baby. As a man, he walks on his two feet. In old age, he walks with the aid of a cane."

The monster was shocked. "That is one of my most difficult puzzles!" she cried. "How did you solve it?"

"Easy," said Oedipus. "I have no fear of death. So I was able to remain calm while thinking it through."

The Sphinx was so ashamed that she threw herself off the boulder. Her stony head hit the ground and broke in two. She was dead! Oedipus had saved Thebes!

The people of Thebes immediately made Oedipus their king. He and Jocasta married. Jocasta never forgot her dear Laius. But she grew to love Oedipus. The couple ruled happily for many years. The city knew peace and prosperity. Its citizens were happy. Until the day a horrible plague fell over the land.

OEDIPUS SOLVES HIS OWN RIDDLE

Oedipus quickly made his way to the oracle at Delphi.

"Why have things gone so wrong?" he asked.

The oracle explained that King Laius's murder had never been properly avenged. "The killer still walks free," the oracle said. "Until that man is punished, Thebes will be cursed."

Oedipus returned to Thebes. He told Jocasta of the oracle's words. Then he asked her for details. "Tell me of your first husband's murder. I must avenge his death."

Jocasta told him everything she knew. She mentioned that her husband had traveled by chariot. That he had died on the road to Delphi. That he had taken just one servant with him. And that the servant had survived. This made Oedipus curious.

"What did Laius look like?" he asked. Oedipus was becoming nervous.

"He was very handsome," Jocasta replied. "Rather like you. His hair was graying. It made him seem much older than he was."

She paused and ruffled Oedipus's hair. "Funny," she continued. "I hadn't noticed, but your hair is turning gray. I suppose you are now about the same age as Laius was when he died."

"What about the servant?" Oedipus pressed. "Does he still work at the palace? May I meet him?"

"No," said Jocasta. "After he told me of Laius's death, he tried to leave town. By that time, the Sphinx was guarding the entrance. I'm afraid he did not solve her riddle."

Oedipus was troubled by Jocasta's answers. All he could think about was his original journey to Thebes. He remembered the man he'd killed. The man with gray hair. The man who was riding toward Delphi with one servant.

"I must leave, Jocasta," Oedipus announced abruptly.

"Where are you going?" she asked.

"I'm off to find Tiresias, the seer. Perhaps he has the answers I need."

"What answers are you seeking?" Jocasta asked.

"I'll tell you when I find out."

Oedipus found Tiresias in the village. Tiresias was very old. He was said to hold the key to all the secrets of the kingdom.

"Please, Tiresias," Oedipus begged. "You must help me."

"I've been expecting you, Oedipus. I knew this day would come."

"Which day?" Oedipus asked.

"The day when you finally figured out your identity."

The seer's words hit Oedipus hard. Everything became clear to him. "Then the oracle's prediction came true!" he shouted. "I murdered my father! And I married my mother!"

"Yes, Oedipus," Tiresias said gently. "It was written on the wind."

"Oh, the agony!" Oedipus cried.

When Jocasta heard this terrible news, she stabbed herself. She lost a lot of blood. But in her mind, she wasn't dying quickly enough. So she hanged herself.

Oedipus found her. His pain overwhelmed him.

"I cannot bear it!" he wailed. "I must never look at another reminder of this life." In his madness, he cut out his eyes with Jocasta's dagger.

Stumbling and insane, Oedipus wandered far, far away from Thebes.

OEDIPUS AND THE ORACLE

The Play

Cast of Characters

Narrator

King Laius

The Oracle

Shepherd

Peasant

Queen Merope

King Polybus

Oedipus

Servant

Queen Jocasta

Adviser 1

Adviser 2

Tiresias

Setting: Ancient Thebes

Act 1

Narrator: A boy was born to King Laius of Thebes. The king consulted the oracle at Delphi.

King Laius: What do I need to know about my son?

The Oracle: You must kill your newborn son. It is the only way to save yourself—and the throne.

Narrator: Laius knew there was no time to waste. After all, an oracle had spoken! So he quickly found a shepherd. He handed him the baby.

King Laius: Take this child. Destroy him at once.

Shepherd: Destroy him? But he is a mere infant, sir.

King Laius: Do you dare question your king?

Shepherd: No, sir.

King Laius: Good!

Narrator: The king walked away without ever looking back.

The shepherd wondered what to do. He did not wish to kill the boy. But he had to obey King Laius. At least in part, he reasoned.

Then he came up with a plan.

Shepherd: I'll tie him to this tree. Perhaps someone will find him. If I leave the field, no one will know where the boy came from. And I won't know who takes him.

Narrator: The shepherd was satisfied with his solution. He tied the baby—by one foot—to the branch of an olive tree. Then he scurried away.

At dusk, a peasant was passing by the olive tree. He heard a baby screaming. He looked and saw the poor boy tied to the tree. The man rushed to untie him.

Peasant: My goodness! What have we here?

Narrator: The man tended to the infant's swollen foot. The child calmed down in the peasant's arms.

Peasant: I think I can help you, dear boy. I come from Corinth. My king and queen long for a baby. They are kind people, and I know they will take you in.

Narrator: The peasant carried the baby to Corinth. He was right—his King Polybus and Queen Merope loved the child instantly.

Queen Merope: What shall we name him?

King Polybus: Let's call him Oedipus. Because of his swollen foot.

Queen Merope: Oedipus it is.

Narrator: The queen sang her son to sleep.

Act II

Narrator: Many years passed. Oedipus grew up happy and strong. Polybus and Merope loved him as their own. They never told him that he was not their son by birth. Soon, however, they wished they had. For someone else beat them to it.

At first, Oedipus was angry with his parents.

Oedipus: Why didn't you tell me?

King Polybus: We didn't think it mattered.

Queen Merope: And you were abandoned—left for dead. We wanted to protect you from the truth. We didn't want you to feel unwanted.

Narrator: Oedipus quickly forgave them.

Oedipus: I am grateful. You have given me such a good life. But I am still curious about my real parents. I must find them. I hope you understand.

Queen Merope: Do what you must, my son.

King Polybus: Go with our blessings.

Narrator: Oedipus knew where to begin his search. He consulted the oracle at Delphi. And he was given a warning.

The Oracle: Do not search for your parents. If you find them, your father will die by your hand. And you will marry your mother.

Oedipus: That's ridiculous!

Narrator: The young man had been taught to believe the oracle. But this time, he just couldn't.

The Oracle: I speak the truth. No good can come from this quest. Leave it in the past.

Oedipus: I would never do the things you suggest.

The Oracle: It is written on the wind.

Oedipus: Then I shall have to change the story.

Narrator: With that, he continued his journey. He was more determined than ever to find his parents—and prove the oracle wrong.

Act III

Narrator: Meanwhile, King Laius was traveling to Delphi. One loyal servant traveled with him. The road was narrow. They met other people here and there. Most were traveling in the opposite direction.

On the second morning, Laius and his servant met a young man driving a chariot. It was Oedipus. The servant called out the king's order.

Servant: Yield to King Laius!

Narrator: Oedipus did not hear the command. So he did not yield. Laius responded by killing one of Oedipus's horses. Oedipus was enraged.

Oedipus: I'll teach you to challenge me!

Narrator: Then he slew the king. When he turned to slay the servant, the servant was gone. He was already hurrying home to Thebes.

Oedipus did not know that he had just murdered a king. He certainly had no idea the king was his own father! So he buried Laius by the side of the road.

Oedipus: Old fool! You should never have killed my horse.

Narrator: The servant arrived back at Thebes the next day. On his journey home, he had spread the news of the king's death. So people from all around were starting to hear about it. He went straight to Queen Jocasta and told her the bad news.

Servant: He is dead, my queen. King Laius is dead.

Queen Jocasta: No!

Narrator: He went on to describe what had happened. He was feeling a bit cowardly for fleeing. So he claimed that a large band of robbers had stopped them. And that he had escaped only after a long fight.

Queen Jocasta: I shall never forget my dear, brave husband.

Narrator: The queen was heartbroken. But she had no time to grieve. Her advisers had arrived with yet more bad news.

Adviser 1: We have an urgent report, Queen Jocasta.

Servant: I'll leave you to your business, my queen. Again, I am so sorry about the king's death.

Queen Jocasta: Thank you for your kind words.

Narrator: The servant left the palace.

Queen Jocasta: Now, then. What urgent news do you bring?

Adviser 2: We are deeply sorry to have to trouble you in your time of sorrow.

Queen Jocasta: Out with it, please. I have little patience right now.

Adviser 1: There is a fierce monster menacing the citizens of Thebes. This monster is called the Sphinx.

Adviser 2: She has the head of a woman and the body of a lion. She heard of the king's death. And she came here right away.

Narrator: The Sphinx had positioned herself atop a huge boulder outside Thebes. She was stopping all people traveling in and out of the city.

Adviser 1: To each traveler, she poses a riddle. If the traveler solves the riddle, the Sphinx grants safe passage. All others are killed on the spot.

Adviser 2: So far, no one has been able to enter or leave Thebes. The riddles are difficult. And the bodies are piling up near the Sphinx's rock.

Queen Jocasta: This is terrible. We must do something to protect the people. But what?

Narrator: The three of them discussed the problem at length. While they talked, Oedipus finally reached Thebes' entrance. Something had drawn him to this great city. He had already been warned about the mighty Sphinx. But he was unafraid.

Oedipus: What is your riddle?

The Sphinx: Which animal travels on four feet in the morning? Two feet at midday? And three feet in the evening?

Narrator: The Sphinx was pleased with her question. She thought it was quite tricky. But Oedipus knew the answer right away.

Oedipus: Man is the animal you describe.
The Sphinx: Explain your response!
Oedipus: He crawls on his hands and knees as a baby. As a man, he walks on his two feet. In old age, he walks with the aid of a cane.

Narrator: The monster was shocked.

The Sphinx: That is one of my most difficult puzzles! How did you solve it?
Oedipus: Easy. I am unafraid to die. So I remained calm while thinking it through.

Narrator: The Sphinx was so ashamed that she threw herself off the boulder. Her stony head broke in two when she hit the ground. She was dead! Oedipus had saved Thebes!

The people of Thebes immediately made Oedipus their king. He and Jocasta married at once. They ruled happily for many years. The city knew peace and prosperity. Its citizens were happy. Until the day when a horrible plague fell over the land.

Oedipus consulted the oracle at Delphi.

Oedipus: Why have things gone so wrong?
The Oracle: King Laius's murder has never been properly avenged. The killer still walks free. Until that man is punished, Thebes will be cursed.

Narrator: Oedipus returned to Thebes. He told Jocasta of the oracle's words. Then he asked her for details.

Oedipus: What happened to your first husband? I must avenge his death.

Narrator: Jocasta told him everything she knew. She mentioned that her husband had traveled by chariot. That he had died on the road to Delphi. That he had taken just one servant with him. And that the servant had survived. This made Oedipus curious.

Oedipus: What did Laius look like?
Queen Jocasta: He was very handsome. Rather like you. His hair was graying. It made him seem much older than he was.

Narrator: The queen paused and ruffled Oedipus's hair. Then she continued.

Queen Jocasta: Funny, I hadn't noticed that your hair is turning gray. I suppose you are now about the same age as Laius was when he died.

Oedipus: What about the servant? Does he still work at the palace? May I meet him?

Queen Jocasta: No. I heard that after he told me of Laius's death, he tried to leave town. By that time, the Sphinx was guarding the entrance. I'm afraid he did not solve her riddle.

Narrator: Oedipus was troubled by Jocasta's answers. All he could think about was his original journey to Thebes. He also remembered the man he'd killed. The man with gray hair. The man who was riding to Delphi with one servant.

Oedipus: I must leave, Jocasta.

Queen Jocasta: Where are you going?

Oedipus: I'm off to find Tiresias, the seer. Perhaps he has the answers I need.

Narrator: Oedipus found Tiresias in the village. Tiresias was very old. He was said to hold the key to all the secrets of the kingdom. Oedipus begged for his help.

Oedipus: Please, Tiresias. You must help me. I have a terrible feeling. Something is not right.

Tiresias: I've been expecting you, Oedipus. I knew this day would come.

Oedipus: Which day?

Tiresias: The day when you finally figured out your identity.

Oedipus: Then the oracle's prediction came true! I murdered my father! And I married my mother!

Tiresias: Yes, Oedipus. It was written on the wind.

Oedipus: Oh, the agony!

Narrator: When Jocasta heard the terrible news, she stabbed and then hanged herself. Oedipus found her. His pain overwhelmed him.

Oedipus: I cannot bear it! I must never look at another reminder of this life.

Narrator: In his madness, Oedipus cut out his eyes with Jocasta's dagger.

Stumbling and insane, he wandered far away from Thebes.

Glossary of Names

Below are descriptions of gods, goddesses, and a few other important names featured in the book.

Adonis a youth who represents nature's decay in winter and its revival in spring

Aphrodite the goddess of love and beauty. She has no parents—she rose from the sea.

Apollo the god of the sun, archery, music, poetry, prophecy, and healing. He is the son of Zeus and the goddess Leto. And he is the twin brother of Artemis.

Artemis the goddess of the moon, hunting, and wildlife. She is the daughter of Zeus and Leto. And she is the twin of Apollo.

Delphi an ancient Greek town. It is the seat of the oracle of Apollo.

Dionysus the god of vegetation and wine. He is the son of Zeus and Semele, a mortal.

Echo one of the mountain nymphs

Eros the god of love. His parents are Aphrodite and Ares, the god of war.

Fates three sisters who spin the thread of human life

Hera the goddess of marriage and childbirth. Her father is Cronus, the lord of the universe. And her mother is Rhea, the goddess of the earth.

Mount Olympus the home of the gods

Narcissus the son of the nymph Leirope and the river-god Cephissus. He is extremely handsome.

Nemesis the goddess of punishment for wrongdoing or undeserved good fortune. She is the daughter of Nyx, or the night.

Nymphs female spirits of a lesser rank than the goddesses. They live in the woods and the water.

Sphinx a monster who has the winged body of a lion and the head of a woman. She poses unanswerable riddles.

Zeus the king of the gods, and the god of heaven and earth. His parents are Cronus and Rhea.